Insights

WOMAN IN

ORATORY, ELOCUTION,

TRAGEDY, DRAMA,

RECITATION, READING,

TABLEAU AND CONVERSATION.

AXIOM PUBLISHING
ISBN 0 947338 17 9

Axiom Publishing
South Australia

contents

The authors of the quotations in this
collection come from many
and varied walks of life,
from all corners of the earth
and are representatives
of many centuries of
human history.
They speak of
universal truths and trivia,
things great and small,
timeless and transitory,
with shouts and whispers.
They share little or nothing in
common,
save the fact they are all women;
speaking life as women.

SELF DISCOVERY

Forgiveness is the key to action and freedom.

Hannah Arendt.

To enjoy freedom we have to control ourselves.

Virginia Woolf.

I think somehow, we learn who we really are and then live with that decision.

Eleanor Roosevelt.

Happiness is not a state to arrive at, but a manner of travelling.

Margaret Lee Runbeck.

I never loved another person the way I loved myself.

Mae West.

They took away what should have been my
eyes,
(But I remembered Milton's Paradise)
They took away what should have been my
ears,
(Beethoven came and wiped away my tears)
They took away what should have been my
tongue,
(But I had talked with God when I was
young)
He would not let them take away my soul,
Possessing that, I still possess the whole.

Helen Keller.

It is not poverty so much as pretence that
harasses a ruined man - the struggle
between a proud mind and an empty purse -
the keeping up a hollow show that must
soon come to an end. Have the courage to
appear poor, and you disarm poverty to its
sharpest sting.

Anna Jameson.

Remember, no one can make you feel
inferior without your consent.
Eleanor Roosevelt.

Love your enemy -
it will drive him nuts.
Eleanor Doan.

I'd rather have roses
on my table than
diamonds on my neck.
Emma Goldman.

Optimism is the faith that leads to
achievement.
Nothing can be done without hope.
Helen Keller.

As long as I live, I will have control over
my being...
Artemisia Gentileschi.

Give and forgive.
Marie Therese Rodet Geoffrin.

Remember that not to be happy
is not to be grateful.
Elizabeth Carter.

Man is wise...when he recognizes no
greater enemy than himself....
Margaret of Navarre

In whatever situation we are placed, our greater or less degree of happiness must be derived from ourselves. Happiness is in a great measure the result of our own dispositions and actions.

Hannah Webster Foster.

Life teaches much, but to all thinking persons it brings ever closer the will of God - not because their faculties decline, but on the contrary, because they increase.

Germaine de Stael.

*Without love, all the merits and power of
man are nothing.*

Margaret of Navarre.

*The harvest of bliss or woe will be
according to the seed-time of this life...*

Bathsua Makin.

*In my view he who goes ahead is always
the one who wins.*

Catherine II of Russia.

*We grow old as soon as we cease to
love and trust.*

Louise Honorine de Choiseul.

*You must often be content to know a thing
is so, without understanding the proof.*

Anna Letitia Barbauld.

True courage consists not in flying from the storms of life, but in braving and steering through them with prudence.
Hannah Webster Foster.

Self-help...that is my whole credo. You cannot sit around like a cupcake asking other people to eat you up and discover your great sweetness and charm. You've got to make yourself more cupcakeable all the time, so that you're a better cupcake to be gobbled up.
Helen Gurley Brown.

Age wins and one must learn to grow old.
Diana Cooper.

One is not born a woman, one becomes one.
Simone de Beauvoir.

If you get through the twilight, you'll live through the night.

Dorothy Parker.

*As I grow older and older
And totter towards the tomb
I find that I care less and less
Who goes to bed with whom.*

Dorothy L. Sayers.

I stand before you tonight in my green chiffon gown, my face softly made up, my fair hair gently waved...the Iron Lady of the Western World. Me? A cold war warrior? Well yes - if that is how they wish to interpret my defence of values and freedoms fundamental to our way of life.

Margaret Thatcher.

I owe nothing to Women's Lib.

Margaret Thatcher.

I cannot and will not cut my conscience to fit this year's fashions.

Lillian Hellman.

*Better by far you should forget and smile
Than that you should remember and be sad.*

Christina Rossetti.

*Since I was twenty-four...there never was
any vagueness in my plans or ideas as to
what God's work was for me.*

Florence Nightingale.

*Risk! Risk anything! Care no more for the
opinions of others, for those voices.
Do the hardest thing on earth for you.
Act for yourself.*

Katherine Mansfield.

Any mind that is capable of a real sorrow is capable of good.

Mrs. Stowe.

*My favorite thing
is to go where
I've never been.*
Diane Arbus.

*Innovators are
inevitably controversial.*
Eva le Gallienne.

What one has to do usually can be done.
Eleanor Roosevelt.

*When you get into a tight place and
everything goes against you, till it seems
you could not hold on a minute longer,
never give up then, for that is just the place
and time that the tide will turn.*
Harriet Beecher Stowe.

*One thing life taught me: if you are
interested, you never have to look for new
interests. They come to you. When you are
genuinely interested in one thing, it will
always lead to something else.*
Eleanor Roosevelt.

*Our needs determine us, as much as we
determine our needs.*
George Eliot.

*What the hell - you might be right, you
might be wrong...but don't just avoid it.*
Katharine Hepburn.

*They are silly. They asked me if I'd mind
having a slight moustache in this film -
and I've got one anyhow.*
                                    Irene Handl.

*Excess of pride can bring the greatest
misery.*
                                    Beatritz de Dia.

*I have learned long since to view people as
they are, and not as I should wish
them to be.*
                                    Catherine II of Russia.

*I cannot read with interest: I am always
reading what I feel and not what I see.*
                                    Julie-Jeanne-Eleonore de Lespinasse.

*At sixty-three years of age, less a quarter,
one still has plans.*
                                    Colette.

COMMUNICATION

*I don't care what is
written about me so long as
it isn't true.*
> Katharine Hepburn.

*Nothing is interesting if
you're not interested.*
> Helen MacInness.

*Good communication is as stimulating as
black coffee, and just as hard to sleep after.*
> Anne Morrow Lindbergh.

*The real art of conversation is not only to
say the right thing in the right place but to
leave unsaid the wrong thing at the
tempting moment.*
> Dorothy Nevill.

So many gods, so many creeds,
So many paths that wind and wind,
When just the art of being kind
Is all the sad world needs.
                              Ella Wheeler Wilcox.

One nice thing about egotists: They don't
talk about other people.
                              Lucille S. Harper.

Chamber music - a conversation between
friends.
Catherine Drinker Bowen.

His voice was as intimate as the rustle of
sheets.
Dorothy Parker.

*Cynicism is an unpleasant way of saying
the truth.*

Lillian Hellman.

*Wit lies in the likeness of things that are
different, and in the difference of things
that are alike.*

Madame de Stael.

*That silence is one of the great arts of
conversation is allowed by Cicero himself,
who says, there is not only an art, but even
an eloquence in it.*

Hannah More.

*When somebody says, "I hope you won't
mind my telling you this," it's pretty certain
that you will.*

Sylvia Bremer.

19

If you have knowledge, let others light their candles at it.

Margaret Fuller.

Tact: Tongue in check.

Sue Dytri.

SOCIETY

Science may have found a cure for most evils; but it has found no remedy for the worst of them all - the apathy of human beings.

Helen Keller.

Society in its full sense ... is never an entity separable from the individuals who compose it.

Ruth Benedict.

Civilization is a method of living, an attitude of equal respect for all men.

Jane Addams.

The strongest bulwark of authority is uniformity; the least divergence from it is the greatest crime.

Emma Goldman.

21

*Tuchman's Law - If power corrupts,
weakness in the seat of power, with its
constant necessity of deals and bribes and
compromising arrangements, corrupts even
more.*

Barbara Tuchman.

*Culture is what your butcher would have if
he were a surgeon.*

Mary Pettibone Poole.

*... persons who would be placed outside the
pale of society with contempt are not those
who would be placed there by another
culture.*

Ruth Benedict.

*Liberty too can corrupt, and absolute
liberty can corrupt absolutely.*

Gertrude Himmelfarb.

Idealists ... foolish enough to throw caution to the winds ... have advanced mankind and have enriched the world.

Emma Goldman.

Since when do you have to agree with people to defend them from injustice?

Lillian Hellman.

Law is a reflection and source of prejudice. It both enforces and suggests forms of bias.

Diane Schulder.

One of the soundest rules I try to remember when making forecasts in the field of economics is that whatever is to happen is happening already.

Sylvia Porter.

*Money is what you'd get
on beautifully without if
only other people weren't
so crazy about it.*
Margaret Case Harriman.

*Kings show their pity in doing justice,
and do justice in showing pity.*
Marie Leszcinska.

*Anyone who thinks there's safety in
numbers hasn't looked at the
stock market pages.*
Irene Peter.

*In conditions of great uncertainty people
tend to predict the events that they want to
happen actually will happen.*
Roberta Wohlstetter.

I have the impression that when we talk so confidently of liberty, we are unaware of the awful servitude ... of poverty when means are so small that there is literally no choice.

Barbara Ward.

It ain't no sin if you crack a few laws now and then, just so long as you don't break any.

Mae West.

I always find that statistics are hard to swallow and impossible to digest. The only one I can ever remember is that if all the people who go to sleep in church were laid end to end they would be a lot more comfortable.

Mrs. Robert A. Taft.

*The trouble with being a breadwinner
nowadays is that the Government is in for
such a big slice.*

Mary McCoy.

*We must have towns that accommodate
different educational groups, different
economic groups, different ethnic groups,
towns where all can live in one place.*

Margaret Mead.

*Today the real test of
power is not capacity to make
war but capacity to prevent it.*

Anne O'Hare McCormick.

*When an individual is kept in a situation of
inferiority, the fact is that he does become
inferior.*

Simone de Beauvoir.

*Social science affirms that a woman's place
in society marks the level of civilization.*
Elizabeth Cady Stanton.

*We have too many high sounding words,
and too few actions that correspond with
them.*
Abigail Adams.

*The source of justice is not vengeance
but charity.*
Bridget of Sweden.

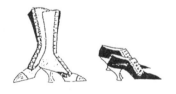

*All goes awry and lawless in the land,
Where power takes the place of justice.*
Margaret of Austria.

*...a Man that wants Money thinks none can
be unhappy that has it....*
                              Susannah Centlivre.

*...the busy part of our
Species, who are so
very intent upon getting
Money, that they lose
the pleasure of spending it.*
                              Mary Davys.

*The worst slavery is that which we
voluntarily impose upon ourselves....*
                              Anna Letitia Barbauld.

*I send you the newspapers; but...they do not
always speak true...*
                              Sarah Bache.

Are we not all links in the great chain of society, some more, some less important, but each upheld by others, throughout the confederated whole?
Hannah Webster Foster.

Scientific progress makes moral progress a necessity; for if man's power is increased, the checks that restrain him from abusing it must be strengthened.
Germaine de Stael.

Freedom is always and exclusively freedom for the one who thinks differently.
Rosa Luxemburg.

As sure as there is a future state of existence, so there is a moral influence to be exerted by every human being according to the measure of his abilities.
Almira Lincoln Phelps.

*When I appear in public people expect me
to neigh, grind my teeth, paw the ground
and swish my tail - none of which is easy.*
                                    Princess Anne.

Nothing succeeds like address.
                                    Fran Lebowitz.

*Someone said that life is a party. You join
after it's started and you leave before it's
finished.*
                                    Elsa Maxwell.

*We don't call it sin today, we call it
self-expression.*
                                    Mary Stocks.

War is the unfolding of miscalculations.
                                    Barbara Tuchman.

The only good government...
is a bad one in a hell of a fright.
Joyce Cary.

Lots of people think they are charitable if
they give away their old clothes and things
they don't want.
Myrtle Reed.

Would that the simple maxim, that honesty
is the best policy, might be laid to heart;
that a sense of the true aim of life might
elevate the tone of politics and trade till
public and private honor become identical.
Margaret Fuller.

No test tube can breed love and affection.
No frozen packet of semen ever read a
story to a sleepy child.

Shirley Williams.

The only people who claim that money is
not important are people who have enough
money so that they are relieved of the ugly
burden of thinking about it.

Joyce Carol Oates.

The message of the media is the
commercial.

Alice Embree.

Well, time wounds all heels.

Jane Ace.

There's so much plastic in this culture that vinyl leopard skin is becoming an endangered synthetic.

Lily Tomlin.

Opportunities are usually disguised as hard work, so most people don't recognize them.

Ann Landers.

A lady is one who never shows her underwear unintentionally.

Lillian Day.

So long as little children are allowed to suffer, there is no true love in this world.

Isadora Duncan.

*What a holler would ensue if people had to
pay the minister as much to marry them as
they have to pay a lawyer to get them a
divorce.*

Clare Trevor.

*As a cousin of mine once said about money,
money is always there but the pockets
change, it is not in the same pockets after a
change, and that is all there is to say
about money.*

Gertrude Stein.

*One must be poor to know the luxury
of giving.*

George Eliot.

She blushed like a well-trained sunrise.

Margaret Halsey.

*'How wonderful it must have been for the
Ancient Britons,'* my mother said once,
*'when the Romans arrived and they could
have a Hot Bath.'*

Katharine Whitehorn.

*My definition (of a philosopher) is of a man
up in a balloon, with his family and friends
holding the ropes which confine him to
earth and trying to haul him down.*

Louisa May Alcott.

CREATIVITY

*Art is the difference between seeing and
just identifying.*
Jean Mary Norman.

*Creativeness often consists of merely
turning up what is already there. Did you
know that right and left shoes were thought
up only a little more than a century ago?*
Bernice Fitz-Gibbon.

*Creative minds always have been known to
survive any kind of bad training.*
Anna Freud.

*If you're going to write, don't pretend to
write down. It's going to be the best you
can do, and it's the fact that it's the best
you can do that
kills you.*
Dorothy Parker.

I find I always have to write something on a steamed mirror.
    Elaine Dundy.

Just how difficult it is to write biography can be reckoned by anybody who sits down and considers just how many people know the real truth about his or her love affairs.
    Rebecca West.

I've always believed in writing without a collaborator, because where two people are writing the same book, each believes he gets all the worries and only half the royalties.
    Agatha Christie.

If writing did not exist, what terrible depressions we should suffer from!
    Sei Shonagon.

I am sorry to hear you are going to publish
a poem. Can't you suppress it?
Elizabeth Holland.

The thriller is the cardinal twentieth
century form. All it, like the twentieth
century, wants to know is: Who's Guilty?
Brigid Brophy.

Creativity varies inversely with the number
of cooks involved in the broth.
Bernice Fitzgibbon.

Pop culture is, perhaps most of all, a
culture of accessible fantasy.
Margot Hentoff.

Some people's food always tastes better
than others',...because one person has
much more life in them...than others...You
have to throw feeling into your cooking.
Rosa Lewis.

God forbid that any book should be
banned. The practice is as indefensible as
infanticide.
Dame Rebecca West.

Another unsettling element in modern art is
that common symptom of immaturity, the
dread of doing what has been done before.
Edith Wharton.

Religion and art spring from the same root
and are close kin. Economics and art are
strangers.
Willa Cather.

*The two most beautiful words in the
English language are 'Cheque Enclosed'.*
Dorothy Parker.

*I ask if he has published anything lately.
He says that his work is not, and never can
be, for publication. Thought passes
through my mind to the effect that this
attitude might with advantage be adopted
by many others.*
E. M. Delafield.

*Some of the new books are so down to
earth they ought to be ploughed under.*
Anne Herbert.

*Acting is not being emotional, but being
able to express emotion.*
Kate Reid.

BEAUTY

I'm tired of all this nonsense about beauty
being only skin-deep. That's deep enough.
What do you want - an adorable pancreas?
                    Jean Kerr.

It's a good thing that beauty is only skin
deep, or I'd be rotten to the core.
                    Phyllis Diller.

...if it were the fashion to go naked, the face
would be hardly observed.
                    Mary Wortley Montagu.

For what is beauty but a sign?
A face hung out, through which is seen
The nature of the goods within.
                    Mary Jones.

Nature gives you the face you have at twenty, but it's up to you to merit the face you have at fifty.

Coco Chanel.

Brevity is the soul of lingerie.

Dorothy Parker.

Why not be oneself? That is the whole secret of a successful appearance. If one is a greyhound, why try to look like a Pekingese?

Edith Sitwell.

It is difficult to see why lace should be so expensive; it is mostly holes.

Mary Wilson Little.

42

LIFE EXPERIENCE

Just because everything is different doesn't mean anything has changed.
Irene Peter.

I believe that anyone can conquer fear by doing the things he fears to do, provided he keeps doing them until he gets a record of successful experiences behind him.
Eleanor Roosevelt.

When choosing between two evils, I always like to try the one I've never tried before.
Mae West.

Callous greed grows pious very fast.
Lillian Hellman.

*What a wonderful life I've had! I only wish
I'd realized it sooner.*

Colette.

A House is not a Home.

Polly Adler.

Ignorance is no excuse - it's the real thing.

Irene Peter.

Ettore's Law - The other line moves faster.

Barbara Ettore.

*Ms. Peter's Law - Today if you're not
confused you're just not thinking clearly.*

Irene Peter.

Life is easier to take than you'd think; all that is necessary is to accept the impossible, do without the indispensable and bear the intolerable.
Kathleen Norris.

A little madness in the Spring
Is wholesome even for the King.
Emily Dickinson.

I loved them because it is a joy to find thoughts one might have, beautifully expressed ...
by someone ...
wiser than oneself.
Marlene Dietrich.

*I refuse to admit I'm more than fifty-two
even if that does make my sons illegitimate.*
Lady Astor.

*I'm not interested in age. People who tell
their age are silly. You're as old as you
feel.*
Elizabeth Arden.

We are tomorrow's past.
Mary Webb.

*Nothing in life is to be feared. It is only to
be understood.*
Marie Curie.

*The only thing I like about rich people is
their money.*
Lady Astor.

I've been rich and I've been poor;
rich is better.

Sophie Tucker.

Security is mortal's chiefest enemy.

Ellen Terry.

The only way to
stop smoking is to
just stop
- no ifs, ands or butts.
Edith Zittler.

If lawyers are disbarred and clergymen
defrocked, doesn't it follow that
electricians can be delighted; musicians
denoted; cowboys deranged; models
deposed; tree surgeons debarked and dry
cleaners depressed?

Virginia Ostman.

Our happiness in this world depends on the
affections we are enabled to inspire.
                                Duchesse de Praslin.

Happiness is a sunbeam which may pass
through a thousanD bosoms without losing
a particle of its original ray;
nay, when it strikes a kindred heart,
like the converged light on a mirror,
it reflects itself
with redoubled brightness.
It is not perfected till it is shared.
                                Jane Porter.

Experience: A comb life gives you after you
lose your hair.
                                Judith Stern.

'Tis easy enough to be pleasant,
When life flows by like a song;
But the man worth while,
Is the man with a smile,
When everything goes dead wrong.

Ella Wheeler Wilcox.

Life has loveliness to sell,
Music like a curve of gold,
Scent of pine trees in the rain,
Eyes that love you, arms that hold,
And for your spirit's still delight,
Holy thoughts that star the night.

Sara Teasdale.

There is always another chance ....
This thing that we call "failure" is not
the falling down, but the staying down.

Mary Pickford.

And though hard be the task,
'Keep a stiff upper lip.'
                              Phoebe Cary.

Eyes of youth have sharp sight, but
commonly not so deep as those of
elder age...
                              Elizabeth I of England.

If practical affairs...cause some objects to
pass through my imagination, these are but
little clouds, like those that pass across the
sun and remove it from our sight for a brief
moment, leaving it bright as before.
                              Marie de L'Incarnation.

A traveller's thoughts in the night
Wander in a thousand miles of dreams.
                              Wang Wei.

*A shadow in the parching sun, and a
shelter in a blustering storm, are of all sea-
sons the most welcome; so a faithfull friend
in time of adversity, is of all other most
comfortable.*

Anne Bradstreet.

*Endeavour to be innocent as a dove,
but as wise as a serpent.*

Ann Fanshawe.

*This may learn
Them that mourn,
To put their grief to flight:
The Spring succeedeth Winter,
And day must follow night.*

Anne Collins.

General notions are generally wrong.
Mary Wortley Montagu.

I give myself sometimes admirable advice,
but I am incapable of taking it.
Mary Wortley Montagu.

People are never so near playing the fool
as when they think themselves wise.
Mary Wortley Montagu.

I am full of faults but I respect and love
virtues.
Elizabeth Aisse.

Minds ripen at very different ages.
Elizabeth Montagu.

It is a wolf who makes the sheep reflect.
Jeanne Poisson Pompadour.

*I am one of the people who love the
why of things.*
Catherine II of Russia.

*...steady as a clock, busy as a bee,
and cheerful as a cricket...*
Martha Washington.

*Eat little at night, open your windows,
drive out often, and look for the good in
things and people... You will no longer be
sad, or bored, or ill.*
Louise Honorine de Choiseul.

Every living creature that comes into the world has something allotted him to perform, therefore he should not stand an idle spectator of what others are doing.
Sarah Kirby Trimmer.

...I have seen too little good come of pride to think of imitating it...
Fanny Burney.

When one gets old one is so thankful to be quiet.
Augusta.

...let us never allow ourselves to depart from truth; it is the beginning of all iniquity.
Elizabeth Hamilton.

It is by surmounting difficulties, not by sinking under them, that we discover our fortitude.
Hannah Webster Foster.

Habit is second nature.
Eliza Leslie.

Make beauty a familiar guest.
Mary Howitt.

It's the good girls who keep the diaries; the bad girls never have the time.
Tallulah Bankhead.

Experience isn't interesting till it begins to repeat itself - in fact, till it does that, it hardly is experience.
Elizabeth Bowen.

*It doesn't matter what you do in the
bedroom as long as you don't do it in the
street and frighten the horses.*
Mrs. Patrick Campbell.

*Our motto: Life is too short to stuff a
mushroom.*
Shirley Conran.

*Some sensible person once remarked that
you spend the whole of your life either in
your bed or in your shoes. Having done the
best you can by shoes and bed, devote all
the time and resources at your disposal to
the building up of a fine kitchen. It will be,
as it should be, the most comforting and
comfortable room in the house.*
Elizabeth David.

We often make people pay dearly for what we think we give them.

Comtesse Diane.

A woman can look both moral and exciting - if she also looks as if it were quite a struggle.

Edna Ferber.

It is better to die on your feet than to live on your knees.

Dolores Ibarruri.

Kissing your hand may make you feel very good, but a diamond and sapphire bracelet lasts for ever.

Anita Loos.

My candle burns at both ends;
It will not last the night;
But, ah, my foes, and oh, my friends -
It gives a lovely light.
Edna St. Vincent Millay.

One more drink and I'll be under the host.
Dorothy Parker.

Where's the man could ease a heart
Like a satin gown.
Dorothy Parker.

Everything tastes better outdoors.
Claudia Roden.

From birth to age eighteen a girl needs
good parents, from eighteen to thirty-five
she needs good looks, from thirty-five she
needs a good personality. From fifty-five
on, she needs good cash.
Sophie Tucker.

*Give a man a free
hand and he'll run
it all over you.*
  Mae West.

*It's not the men in my life, it's the life
in my men that counts.*

Mae West.

*The best careers advice to give to the young
is 'Find out what you like doing best and
get someone to pay you for doing it'.*
Katherine Whitehorn.

*Well! some people talk of morality, and
some of religion, but give me a little
snug property.*
Maria Edgeworth.

*The best way to get the better of temptation
is just to yield to it.*
Clementina Stirling Graham.

No time like the present.
Mrs. Manley.

After all, tomorrow is another day.
Margaret Mitchell.

*...But warm, eager, living life - to be rooted
in life - to learn, to desire to know, to feel,
to think, to act. That is what I want.
And nothing less.
That is what I must try for.*
Katherine Mansfield.

By the bye, as I must leave off being young,
I find many Douceurs in being a sort of
Chaperon for I am put on the Sofa near the
fire & can drink as much wine as I like.
                                                    Jane Austen.

...A letter from a lady who has described
me in a French newspaper - 'a noble lady
with a shock of white hair' - Lord, are we
as old as all that? I feel about six and a
half.
                                                    Virginia Woolf.

One should never be sorry one has
attempted something new -
never, never, never.
                                                    Sybil Thorndike.

Going into business for
yourself, becoming an
entrepreneur is the modern-day
equivalent of pioneering
on the old frontier.
                                                    Paula Nelson.

*When we depend less on industrially
produced consumer goods, we can live in
quiet places. Our bodies will become
vigorous; we discover the serenity of living
with the rhythms of the earth. We cease
oppressing one another.*
Alicia Bay Laurel.

*I must say I hate money
but it's the lack of it I hate most.*
Katherine Mansfield.

*The best impromptu speeches are the ones
written well in advance.*
Ruth Gordon.

*It is my melancholy fate to like so many
people I profoundly disagree with and often
heartily dislike people who agree with me.*
Mary Kingsley.

I believe in the total depravity of inanimate things...the elusiveness of soap, the knottiness of strings, the transitory nature of buttons...

Katharine Ashley.

Since when was genius found respectable?
Elizabeth Barrett Browning.

Anyone who makes a lot of money quickly must be pretty crooked - honest pushing away at the grindstone never made anyone a bomb.

Marilyn Rice-Davies.

Let no one till his death be called unhappy.
Measure not the work until the day's out
and the labour done.
Elizabeth Browning.

No one ever pruned me. If you have been
sunned through and through like an apricot
on a wall from your earliest days, you are
oversensitive to any withdrawal of heat.
Margot Asquith.

Success to me is having
ten honeydew melons
and eating only the
top half of each one.
Barbra Streisand.

Do you know how helpless you feel if you
have a full cup of coffee in your hand and
you start to sneeze?
Jean Kerr.

One learns in life to keep silent and draw one's own confusions.
                              Cornelia Otis Skinner.

I'll not listen to reason...Reason always means what someone else has got to say.
                              Mrs. Gaskell.

What strange impulse is it which induces otherwise trustful people to say they like music when they do not, and thus expose themselves to hours of boredom?
                              Agnes Repplier.

I feel about airplanes the way I feel about diets. It seems to me that they are wonderful things for other people to go on.
                              Jean Kerr.

When I was young I was frightened I might bore other people, now I'm old I am frightened they will bore me.

Ruth Adam.

Perhaps the straight and narrow path would be wider if more people used it.

Kay Ingram.

The character of a child is already plain, even in its mother's womb...
If people ask me when I began to dance I reply, 'In my mother's womb, probably as a result of the oysters and champagne - the food of Aphrodite'.

Isadora Duncan.

Variety is the soul of pleasure.

Aphra Behn.

A diamond is the only kind of ice that keeps a girl warm.

Elizabeth Taylor.

Give the neighbor's kids an inch and they'll take a yard.

Helen Castle.

I feel a recipe is only a theme, which an intelligent cook can play each time with a variation.

Madame Benoit.

FAMILY & CHILDREN

*The best way to keep children home is to
make the home atmosphere pleasant -
and let the air out of the tires.*
                                    Dorothy Parker.

*We must have ... a place where children
can have a whole group of adults they
can trust.*
                                    Margaret Mead.

*If a child lives with approval, he learns to
live with himself.*
                                    Dorothy Law Nolte.

*Everyone is the
Child of his past.*
    Edna G. Rostow.

No matter how many communes anybody invents, the family always creeps back.
Margaret Mead.

Instant availability without continuous presence is probably the best role a mother can play.
Lotte Bailyn.

No one without the experience knows the anguish which children can cause and yet be loved.
Elisabeth of Braunschweig.

Oh, to be only half as wonderful as my child thought I was when he was small, and only half as stupid as my teenager now thinks I am.
Rebecca Richards.

A mother's love!
If there be one thing pure,
Where all beside is sullied,
That can endure,
When all else passes away;
If there be aught
Surpassing human deed or word, or
thought,
It is a mother's love.
Marchioness de Spadara.

...think always that, having the child at
your breast, and having it in your arms,
you have God's blessing there.
Elizabeth Clinton.

But birds have always the good nature to
teach their young ones, and so must you.
Margaret Godolphin.

Only a mother knows a mother's fondness.
Mary Wortley Montagu.

70

...childhood is never troubled with foresight...
Fanny Burney.

'The school may do much; but alas for the child where the instructor is not assisted by the influences of home!'
Hannah Farnham Lee.

A food is not necessarily essential just because your child hates it.
Katherine Whitehorn.

Your responsibility as a parent is not as great as you might imagine. You need not supply the world with the next conqueror of disease or major motion picture star. If your child simply grows up to be someone who does not use the word 'collectible' as a noun, you can consider yourself an unqualified success.

Fran Lebowitz.

When the loo paper gets thicker and the writing paper thinner it's always a bad sign, at home.

Nancy Mitford.

Cleaning your house while your kids are still growing is like shovelling the walk before it stops snowing.

Phyllis Diller.

DEATH

The rain has such a friendly sound
To one who's six feet underground.
                    Edna St. Vincent Millay.

When I am dead, my dearest,
Sing no sad songs for me.
                    Christina Rossetti.

I gave my life to learning how to live.
Now that I have organized it all ...
It is just about over.
                    Sandra Hochman.

This is my death ... and it will profit me to
understand it.
                    Anne Sexton.

ENVIRONMENT

*The most alarming of all man's assaults
upon the environment is the contamination
of air, earth, rivers, and sea ... this
pollution is for the most part irrecoverable.*
Rachel Carson.

*We won't have a society if we destroy the
environment.*
Margaret Mead.

 *Any interference with
nature is damnable.
Not only nature but also
the people will suffer.*

Anahario
(wife of Grey Owl.)

Anything we can conceive, we can achieve -
the most underdeveloped territory in the
world is under our scalps, and I would that
we have calluses on our minds but not
bunions on our countryside!
Dorothy M. Carl.

This could be such a beautiful world.
Rosalind Welcher.

Only within the moment of time represented
by the present century has one
species - man - acquired significant power
to alter the nature of his world.
Rachel Carson.

*Animals are such agreeable friends - they
ask no questions, they pass no criticisms.*
                      Marian Evans.

*I am more and more convinced that man is
a dangerous creature....*
                    Abigail Adams.

*Along the shore the willows
Wait for their Spring green.*
              Sun Yun-feng.

*The universe, how vast! exceeding far
The bounds of human thought; millions of
suns,
With their attendant worlds moving
around
Some common centre, gravitation strange!
Beyond the power of finite minds to scan!*
             Almira Lincoln Phelps.

*Man thinks of himself as a creator instead
of a user, and this delusion is robbing him,
not only of his natural heritage,
but perhaps of his future.*

Helen Hoover.

*The chestnut's proud, and the lilac's pretty
The poplar's gentle and tall,
But the plane tree's kind to the poor
dull city -
I love him best of all!*

Edith Nesbit.

*I like trees because they seem more
resigned to the way they have to live than
other things do.*

Willa Cather.

EDUCATION

*The first idea that the child must acquire, in
order to be actively disciplined, is that of
the difference between good and evil; and
the task of the educator lies in seeing that
the child does not confound good with
immobility, and evil with activity.*

Maria Montessori.

*Journalism is the ability to meet the
challenge of filling space.*

Rebecca West.

The brain is as strong as its weakest think.

Eleanor Doan.

*I got all the schooling any actress needs.
That is, I learned to write enough to
sign contracts.*
Hermione Gingold.

*It does not make much difference what a
person studies - all knowledge is related,
and the man who studies anything, if he
keeps at it, will become learned.*
Hypatia.

*When I step into this library, I cannot
understand why I ever step out of it.*
Marie de Sevigne.

*True knowledge consists in knowing things,
not words.*
Mary Wortley Montagu.

Even at eighteen, a mentally voracious
young woman cannot live entirely upon
scenery.

Vera Brittain.

Prejudices, it is well known, are most
difficult to eradicate from the heart whose
soil has never been loosened or fertilized by
education; they grow there, firm as weeds
among stones.

Charlotte Bronte.

Better build schoolrooms for 'the boy'
Than cells and gibbets for 'the man'.

Eliza Cook.

The only inequalities that matter begin in
the mind. It is not income levels but
differences in mental equipment that keep
people apart, breed feelings of inferiority.

Jacquetta Hawkes.

Knowledge is not given as gift, but through study...
                                    Laura Cereta.

To be able to be caught up into the world of thought - that is being educated.
                                    Edith Hamilton.

FRIENDSHIP, LOVE,
MARRIAGE

*I never hated a man enough to give him his
diamonds back.*
Zsa Zsa Gabor.

*An archeologist is the best husband any
woman can have; the older she gets, the
more interested he is in her.*
Agatha Christie.

*If love makes the world go 'round,
Why are we going to outer space?*
Margaret Gilman.

...who would live and not love?
                              Rachel Russell.

*My shattered heart grew precious
in your sight.*
                              Juana Ines de la Cruz.

*Friendship's a noble name, 'tis love
refined.*
                              Susannah Centlivre.

*...I could never love where I could not
respect.*
                              Charlotte Elizabeth Aisse.

*The hardest thing in the world
Is to reveal a hidden love.*
                              Ho Shuang-ch'ing.

*Love...generally hurries us on without
Consideration...*
                                    Mary Hearne.

*I count time by your absence; I have not
seen you all morning, and is it not an age
since then?*
                                    Peg Woffington.

*Certainly, my dear, friendship is a mighty
pretty invention, and, next to love, gives of
all things the greatest spirit to society.*
                                    Frances Brooke.

The balm of life, a kind and faithful friend.
                                    Mercy Otis Warren.

Ah! how the mind weakens when one loves.
                                    Julie-Jeanne-Eleonore de Lespinasse.

84

The logic of the heart is absurd.
Julie-Jeanne-Eleonore de Lespinasse.

For friendship soars above low rules
Annis Stockton.
...a friend was never chosen.
Anna Letitia Barbauld.

To a heart formed for friendship and affection the charms of solitude are very short-lived...
Fanny Burney

There is no magician like Love...
Marguerite Blessington.

If ever a woman feels proud of her lover, it is when she sees him as a successful public speaker.

Harriet Beecher Stowe.

Though God hath raised me high, yet this I count the glory of my crown: that I have reigned with your loves.

Queen Elizabeth I of England.

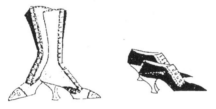

Stephon kissed me in the spring,
Robin in the fall,
And Colin only looked at me
And never kissed at all.

Stephon's kiss was lost in jest,
Robin's lost in play,
But the kiss in Colin's eyes
Haunts me night and day.

Sara Teasdale.

Some pray to marry the man they love,
My prayer will somewhat vary;
I humbly pray to Heaven above
That I love the man I marry.

Rose Pastor Stokes.

I will uphold you, trunk and shoot and
flowering sheaf
And I will hold you, root, and fruit and
falling leaf.

E. J. Scovell.

Chains do not hold a marriage together. It
is threads, hundreds of tiny threads which
sew people together through the years.
That is what makes a marriage
last - more than passion or even sex!

Simone Signoret.

*Before marriage a man will lie awake all
night·thinking about something you said;
after marriage he will fall asleep before
you have finished saying it.*
                              Helen Rowland.

*The reason that husbands and wives do not
understand each other is because they
belong to different sexes.*
                              Dorothy Dix.

Platonic love is love from the neck up.
                     Thyra Samter Winslow.

*She always believed in the old adage,
'Leave them while you're looking good.'*
                              Anita Loos.

When she raises her eyelids it's as if she were taking off all her clothes.

Colette.

We should not let the grass grow on the path of friendship.

Marie Therese Rodet Geoffrin.

Love thy neighbor as thyself, but choose your neighborhood.

Louise Beal.

Platonic friendship: The interval between the introduction and the first kiss.

Sophie Irene Loeb.

Never go to bed mad. Stay up and fight.
Phyllis Diller.

Being married is a value: it is bread and butter, but it may make one less able to provide the cake.
Naomi Mitchison.

A liaison of seven years is like following a husband to the colonies; when you come back no one recognizes you and you've forgotten how to wear your clothes properly.
Colette.

To have a good enemy, choose a friend: he knows where to strike.
Diane de Poitiers.

SPIRITUAL

Just about any dream
Grows stonger
If you hold on
A little longer.

Margo Gina Hart.

I've always said my daily prayers
For I thought that I should pray.
And so I learned the routine ones
And said them every day.

But now it seems as I grow wiser
With the coming of each day
And I am substituting "Thanks" for
"Please"
When it's time for me to pray.

Elizabeth Smith.

...in all human affairs there are things both
certain and doubtful, and both are equally
in the hands of God.

Isabella I.

91

God, give me sympathy and sense,
And help me keep my courage high;
God, give me calm and confidence,
And - please - a twinkle in my eye.
Amen.

Margaret Bailey.

The Good Samaritan, when he came upon
the man who had fallen among thieves,
did not ask him to what denomination he
belonged, but put him on his ass
and took him to an inn.

Katherine Zell.

Oh Lord, in thee have I hoped, and into thy
hands I commit my spirit.

Mary, Queen of Scots.

In my end is my beginning.

Mary, Queen of Scots.

Science conducts us, step by step, through the whole range of creation, until we arrive, at length, at God.
Marguerite of Valois.

[God's] love is like the evening and morning raine upon the earth...
Ann Wheathill.

This life is like an inn, in which the soul spends a few moments on its journey.
Christina of Sweden.

The Deity is not confined to temples made with hands.
Hannah Webster Foster.

*God has made man to be a
brother to man, if we will
only place confidence
in each other.*
Hannah Farnham Lee.

*To understand God's thoughts we must
study statistics, for these are the measure
of his purpose.*
Florence Nightingale.

*If you think about it, you will find that there
is no meaning in life if you are estranged
from God.*
Catherine Bramwell-Booth.

*We must try to love without imagining. To
love the appearance in its nakedness
without interpretation. What we love then
is God.*
Simone Weil.